TO: Britney

Thank you for your support!
God has more for you! keep
going!

Rosa Rek

GET YOUR FIGHT BACK

STRATEGIES TO WIN THE BATTLES OF LIFE

ROSCOE ROBINSON

CONTENTS

PREFACE

The Webster dictionary describes fighting as "taking part in a violent struggle involving the exchange of physical blows or the use of weapons." When you were a kid, did you ever have a neighborhood or school bully who always picked on the weakest or smallest kid? Some of you right now are being bullied by the enemy to shrink back and to stop fighting for the life that God wants you to have. In this book, I want to encourage you and give you strategies on how to get back up from the defeat that the enemy has tried to cause you. By telling you that this is how it will always be.

We all have a fight deep down inside of us. Life may have knocked you on the ropes through health issues, divorces, loss of jobs, rejection, hurt, and all types of pain that we go through in this life. I encourage you that there is hope, you can get back in the ring and win in this fight of life every day. You may feel like you are at your wit's end and that you will never get out of that place. I want to assure you that there is victory on the other side of this test and the struggle you may be facing now in your life. Now, let us journey together on how to get your fight back.

CHAPTER 1

PREPARATION

When it comes to fighting, most of us have seen boxing matches throughout the years that have been training grounds for the big fight. The adversary loves to bluff by throwing hard blows that appear to be the big fight so that he can wear you out before his final sneak attack! In a fight, two opponents are trying to win, and eventually whoever wins gets the prize (money). However, on the way to your destiny day, there is a preparation phase that each fighter must go through. The preparation takes discipline, focus, and no distractions.

The Bible says, *"For we wrestle not against flesh and blood, but against principalities, against powers, against the rulers of the darkness of this world, against spiritual wickedness in high places"* (Ephesians 6:12). We are truly in a real war as believers. We have an enemy who will do everything in his power to stop our progress. Have you ever been on fire for the things of God, reading His Word, fellowshipping with other believers, praying, and serving faithfully? Then suddenly, bam! Out of nowhere your fire and momentum die and you are wondering where the heck did this come from. We have an adversary *".... who is like a roaring lion seeking whom he may devour"* (1 Peter 5:8). His main goal is to not let us ever find out what our identity in Christ is. He will keep us in little bitty fights with each other and with ourselves to stop us from fulfilling our destiny. The Word says, *"He who is in you is greater than he who is in the world"* (1 John 4:4). You have the greater one living inside of you! You have power that is inside of you!

"For the weapons of our warfare are not carnal but might in God for pulling down strongholds" (2 Corinthians 10:4). Now, what is a stronghold? I'm glad you asked! A stronghold is a negative thought pattern that has shaped our mindsets over a period, usually starting as a child. Some examples of that include negative words spoken by friends, family, and/ or those close to us. For instance, "You are going to be just like your no-good daddy." "You don't look nice as her or him." "I can't believe you did that! "It was all luck." These negative words affect us subconsciously. You find yourself going through life feeling like you are stuck. It may even feel like there is this imaginary line that keeps you from moving forward in your career and relationships in your life. Know without a doubt that God has your back. Fight those negative thoughts and speak God's word over yourself! "... Fearfully and wonderfully made!" That is what God has spoken concerning you! (Psalm 139:14).

In preparation for a fight, one must go into intense training. The training consists of daily cardio, lifting weights, fighting techniques, and most of all mental resilience and endurance. Those who are champions in a fight always win in their minds long before they step foot in the ring. Every day they do the same thing, being consistent day after day, and eventually, it produces results. What is that one thing that is stopping you from getting up to fight? God has much for you to do on the earth and He is looking for those who will have the tenacity to move forward no matter how difficult it may seem. In my life personally, there have been several fights I have had to take on when all odds were against me.

When I was seventeen, I had a traumatic experience that knocked the wind out of me. On Christmas Day of the year 2007, I found my father dead on the couch of a heart attack. I was mad at God, and this led to a downhill spiral of depression, drinking, sexual promiscuity, and smoking weed as I tried to block out the pain. This lasted about a year and a half until I came out of that dark place. I had to fight to find joy again and a reason to keep going.

After this experience, the enemy planted a seed in me that if I got too close to people that they will leave me. This made having relationships especially with father figures extremely difficult in my life. All of this was a lie from the enemy! There are people out there who will not walk out on me and will love me unconditionally.

Some of you may be facing the same thing, fighting to stay close to people who genuinely care and love you. You cannot trust everyone but there are people out there who have the best interests and intentions for you. To transform our minds, we must be anchored in the Word of God. The Word says to, *"... fight the good fight of faith"* (1 Timothy 6:12), you must make up in your mind that you are going to fight the old thought patterns that have been engrained in your mind for years. One of the most important pieces of the armor of God we must put on is the helmet of salvation that protects our minds. Our minds are extremely critical in this battle that we are in. Every action we take in life is connected to a thought first.

The Bible says, *"As a man thinketh in his heart so is he"* (Proverbs 23:7). What do you think about yourself when you hear those thoughts of "you will never make it," "you might as well quit and stop that", "no one in your family has done this and that". These are all lies from the enemy. The Bible says the enemy is" a liar and the father of it" (John 8:44).

When preparing for war, have you ever seen a general give a private in the trenches milk and cookies? He is training him to fight in all types of conditions. In life, we will have to face all types of conditions to continue to keep moving forward. You may be in a season of rest and peace when everything seems like it is going well. This is the time for you to build your spiritual muscles and stamina by reading the Word, praying in the spirit, and connecting with other like-minded believers. There also may be a season where things are somewhat good and somewhat not good. You may feel like you are on a rollercoaster emotionally: one day up and one day down. Now, this is a time to really focus because the enemy may try to throw an uppercut out of nowhere in your life. After all, you have not been consistently training and preparing yourself.

The next season it feels like what Muhammad Ali called the "Rope-a -Dope," the enemy has you on the ropes and you do not know how you are going to get out of this situation. The "rope-a-dope" is used to describe strategies in which one contender draws non-injuring offensive punches to let the opponent tire themselves out. This gives the former the opportunity to then execute devastating offensive maneuvers to help them win. Have you ever felt like you have been in a situation where the enemy has tried to tire you out? You feel like all hell is breaking loose in your life and things are falling apart around you but remember all things are working together for your good! (Romans 8:28). No matter how difficult this season may be do not stop praying and keep fighting! You are almost to the finish line.

Sometimes, God may ask you to do strange things to win a battle that you may be facing. A similar battle parallel to the story of the walls of Jericho in the Bible. Joshua had them walk around the walls seven times and the walls eventually fell. They probably thought to themselves, "Lord, really? Do you want us to do this? Will we win this battle? Lo and behold, they let out a shout of praise! Praise is the atomic bomb of spiritual warfare! Praise counter attacks every weapon formed against you! Praise is the act of magnifying the name of our Great Jehovah over the threats, and efforts of our enemies!

In the Old Testament before a battle, the army would let Judah to go first which means praise to confuse the enemy. The enemy is not looking for you to praise God when everything around you is telling you to be silent and you are thinking to yourself how in the world will I come out of this situation. What is endurance? When you think of endurance, you may think of a Boston Marathon runner who runs over three hours to win the race. As a believer, we are running for an eternal prize that Christ wants to give us. Endurance is developed over time. It does not just happen instantly.

When I ran track, our coach would time us for endurance tests at the beginning of the season to measure where our physical condition was. Three months from then, we should have improved in our stamina, jumps, and times. If we did not improve, the evidence of not training adequately or not eating properly were going to show up when the tests came. Tests come in our lives as believers to show us what we are made of. Will this test come to break us, or will this test come and make us stronger? The Word says that we are surrounded by a cloud of witnesses that are cheering us on to keep going to keep fighting the good fight of faith no matter how tough it may get. The Word says those who "endure to the end will be saved," (Matthew 24:13).

Endurance is built through trials and tribulations. It's the good and bad seasons of our life when we feel like

God may have left us or we feel counted out. Take for example when a person enlists in Bootcamp, they must leave the civilian life behind and become everything that the military wants them to be. Their old life is gone and now they are in this new life in the military. There is even a new language required in the new environment, everything about them must change if they want to pass the course and pass the test to get out of Bootcamp. Endurance may take many restless nights where you feel like all hope is lost and you want to throw in the towel. I want to encourage you not to give up when you are on a verge of a breakthrough in your life. Endure and as my grandma would say, "Go ahead and see what the end is going to be."

Prayer: *"Lord, help me to prepare for the battles of life. Father, you said, Greater is He that is within me than he that is in the world. Help me never to waste the preparation time that you are taking me through so that I can be victorious in every area of my life. I am more than a conqueror! Thank you that preparation time is never wasted time on this journey of life. In Jesus' name, Amen."*

Reflection: What areas in my life do I need to be better prepared?

_____

_____

_____

_____

_____

_____

_____

CHAPTER 2

KNOW YOUR AUTHORITY

We must realize as believers we have authority. Authority means "the power or right to give orders, make decisions, and enforce obedience." Once you realize who you are and who you belong to; your fight becomes easier. Because we have weapons as believers to fight off the enemy and he loses whenever we do not let our own will get in the way. We have the Word of God which is our ammunition as Jesus did when He was tempted in the wilderness. He always replied with, "It is written", not I said this and that. The place that we can get messed up in this fight is fighting in our own strength and not relying on the power of God that says, "When we are weak, He is strong" (2 Corinthians 12:10).

The Word of God is sharper than any two-edged sword. He said that His Word will not return to Him void without accomplishing what it was set to do. So, the Word that God has given to you will come to pass. Also, we have angels who are ministering spirits that excel in strength for believers (Psalms 103:20). You can command your angels to be loosed to get your healing and financial blessings. Also, praying in the spirit is another weapon of mass destruction against the enemy. When we pray in the spirit, we speak mysteriously and release utterances that are unknown to man but known to God (1 Corinthians 14:18). As believers, we have several weapons against the enemy of our lives. We have a God who's seated in heavenly places; that means we fight from a position of victory and not defeat.

In the sixth chapter of Ephesians, the Apostle Paul describes each area of the whole armor of God. *"Put on the whole armor of God, that you may be able to stand against the wiles of the devil"* (Ephesian 6:11). But not once does he say that God will put this armor on for you. YOU have the responsibility to be strong in the Lord and put on the armor every day to withstand the enemy. James 4:7 says, *"Submit to God, resist the devil and he will flee."* That takes action on your behalf as a believer. Stand your ground and the enemy will flee! Ephesians 4:21-24 says, *"if indeed you have heard Him and have been taught by Him, as the truth is in Jesus: that you put off, concerning your former conduct, the old man which grows corrupt according to the deceitful lusts, and be renewed in the spirit of your mind, and that you put on the new man which was created according to God, in true righteousness and holiness."* We are the ones in authority and the Holy Spirit will do the work in us. The enemy wants us to not put off the old man and to fight in the flesh and not the spirit. Once we know our authority the enemy is no match to us any longer.

Prayer: *"Father, I thank you that you have given me power and authority as a believer. You said in your Word in (Luke 10: 19) 'Behold, I give you the authority to trample on serpents and scorpions, and over all power of the enemy, and nothing shall by any means hurt you.' Help me to understand who I am in you and not rely on my own strength and understanding but your power working through me. You said in your Word 'not by might, nor by power, but by your spirit' (Zechariah 4:6). Father, I will use my authority when the enemy tries to tell me lies about myself. Your Word has the final say! In Jesus' name, I pray, Amen."*

Reflection: In what areas of my life am I not exercising my authority as a believer?

_____

_____

_____

_____

_____

CHAPTER 3

KNOW WHO YOUR TARGET IS

I n a boxing match, there are rounds that each fighter must go through. It is whoever gets the most punches or knockout that will win. The boxer always looks for the weak areas of the opponent to catch them off guard to sneak in a punch. Paul tells us in 1 Corinthians 9:26, *"Therefore I run thus: not with uncertainly. Thus, I fight: not as one who beats the air."* Our target is never people or situations, rather our target is the enemy. Therefore, we must ask God for discernment of what spirit is in operation in this situation or through this person. As the Word says in Ephesian 6:12, *"We do not wrestle against flesh and blood."*

We have all likely had a conflict with another person at some point in our lives, and we probably responded verbally or physically to their aggression (or they responded to ours if we were the instigator). It is typical human behavior to respond in this way. If they say something to you, you reply to them too; if they push you, then you push them back. Such a behavioral response is expected from most people because our view of the world is dominated by how we see things. Our natural tendency is to understand the world by what we see with our eyes. As believers, we must realize who we are fighting is not a person, but a spirit that is working through that person. The enemy wants to kill you in life, to not let you get back up and catch your breath. *"A righteous man falls down seven times and rise again,"* (Proverbs 24:16). You can and will get back up and keep fighting. Some of you will be the first in your family to complete a college degree, start a business, and become a doctor or lawyer. You have what it takes no matter what the naysayers may say.

In life, there will always be people with a negative attitude. Also, another area you must target in this fight is your self-esteem. Self-esteem is the way you feel about yourself when no one is around. It does not come from having titles, positions, money, and all the material things that you want. But who does God say you are? When you go to sleep at night how do you feel about yourself? Are you wearing a mask or have people ever met the real you? The enemy will do everything in his power to make you always have low self-esteem. This is an area I really struggled with as a teen and even in my adult life. I was always looking to be accepted by my peers, church members, and people around me. I was a great athlete in school and excelled and always wanted the approval of people which led to an identity crisis when I stopped playing sports. I struggled to finding who was I? It led me to fight with God to know who I was without the approval of man. It took years of tearing those lies of the enemy down. Then I finally realized I was accepted by God, not based on my performance, but because He loves me, and I am His son.

Prayer: *Father, help me to realize that I am not fighting flesh and blood when I have battles in my life. Help me to have a level of discernment in the spirit that I will know the schemes of the enemy that is trying to operate in my life. Father, you said in your Word, "Lest Satan should take advantage of us; for we are not ignorant of his devices" (2 Corinthians 2:11). Help me to see people the way that you see them so that I can walk boldly as a believer knowing the target is not people. In Jesus' name, Amen.*

Reflection: What areas in my life do I need to focus on the spiritual target?

_____

_____

_____

_____

_____

CHAPTER 4

SURROUND YOURSELF WITH TRUTH

P hysical pains or emotional pains are the triggers that the enemy send when you are in a fight. He will try to taunt you without mercy to convince you that there is no light at the end of the tunnel. He will also trick you into believing that there is no relief or no potential to life. You need to acknowledge the situation but remember to tell yourself the truth and memorize it! You may have to get index cards and write scriptures or affirmations. For example, it could be as simple as "This WILL end!" You need to confess the Word each day to remind yourself and circumstances that it will not be permanent.

You may be battling sickness in your body and even though the symptoms are showing each day you must remind yourself that, "By His stripes, I am healed!" "Sickness you have no place in my life or the life of my loved ones in Jesus' name!" A funny thing about emotions is, they change. Just like children one moment they want to watch a movie and the other second, they want ice cream. We are called in the Word to be child-like but not childish. We must remember that the Word is the final say in our lives no matter what has broken loose in our lives. The enemy will come to you when you are at your weakest point and tell you lies because he is the father of lies and there is no truth in him. He will say, "You will not make it out of this, everyone around you is getting married and you are still single, look at what you have done, and you will not make it out of this situation". The Word says, *"You shall know the truth and the truth shall make you free",* (John 8:32). And whoever the Son sets free will be free indeed.

As a believer, freedom is your portion in every aspect of your life as the Word reiterates in (1 John 1:3). *"I wish above ALL THINGS that you would prosper and be in good health even as your soul prospers."* That is a promise as a believer you have the right to be prosperous in every area of your life. Your finances, job, marriage, children, health, all of it are blessed by God. Another thing about emotions, they will never tell you the consequences of the action you are about to take. They always show you the immediate gratification and not the long-term effect the choice could have. Many of you are right on the edge of walking into your Promised Land. I love the story of children of Israel who complained and complained when they were right near the Promised Land. They liked their old lives better which was slavery, but the enemy made it seem like it was better back in Egypt where they were killed and worked long hours as slaves. What has the enemy said to you during this season to make you feel like your old life was better than now? I want to remind you that all that is back there is death, and your Father has so many better things for you in the future.

Prayer: *"Father, I thank you that your Word is truth. Lord, help me during this difficult time to rely on your strength and not mine. You said when I am weak, then you are strong. It does not feel like I am strong, but it does not matter how I feel but what I know and believe about you and who you are. In Jesus' name, Amen."*

Reflection: What areas in my life do I need truth? What areas in my life have I been believing a lie?

CHAPTER 5

SURROUND YOURSELF WITH HOPE

In the dictionary, hope is "a feeling of expectation and desire for a certain thing to happen." When you are in a fight in your life, you must remind yourself that things will change. The Lord says, *"My thoughts are not your thoughts nor are your ways my ways"* (Isaiah 55:8). Sometimes, we do not understand things we go through and how we are going to ever get out of the situation. Also, to find hope during this fight of your life you may have to get inspirational scriptures that you can paste in your room, in your car, and wherever you may see it to speak to your situation. Moreover, you may have a positive song that you listen to over and over to feed your spirit and not your situation.

You must magnify God in the situation and say that "there is nothing impossible with God." What is something in your life that God cannot do? He ALWAYS comes through no matter how small or big the problem may be. Also, as a good Father, He always gives good gifts to His sons and daughters. Surround yourself with faith-filled people who are going to encourage you in this place you are at now. As the old saying goes "misery loves company" and it is so true during these trying times we go through in life. Do any of you have a friend or acquaintance who loves to come around and just add fuel to the fire during your difficult times? My advice to you is to get rid of them immediately during this time of your life.

I remember when I was about to be a senior in college and had lost my Federal Pell Grant money which I was going to use to pay for my apartment and living expenses for my senior year. I did not know what I was going to do. The only thing I could do was trust God and pray that a miracle would happen. I had two months for this miracle to come through. So, I began to activate my faith and say, "Lord I am your child and your son, and you said that you will supply all my needs." "You desire for me to finish school and I will finish school next year."

The enemy was whispering in my ear daily you will never get the money. The total amount of money was $7,000. I continued to play worship music of hope in my ears and read the Word daily. Two weeks later, a family back home found out about my situation and paid for all my senior year of living expenses. I was in a fight, and I had to realize that I could stand under the pressure. That is one of the tactics of the enemy is to get you in a situation where the pressure feels unbearable that you are going to break down. But I want to remind you that you will not break under pressure! That you are a mighty warrior! You must get into your spirit a fight that says, "I will get through this." On the other side of this is a future of hope that God has for you. Trust Him!

Prayer: *Lord, I thank you that my hope is found in you. You are a sure foundation and all blessings and good things come from you. Lord, I thank you that I can trust your ways and not my ways and thoughts. Thank you for preparing a great future for me according to Jeremiah 29:11. I will continue to trust you Lord and put ALL my hope in you even when things aren't going the way I want them to go. In Jesus' name, Amen.*

Reflection: What things in my life am I hoping for? Who are hope killers in my life that I need to disconnect from within this season?

CHAPTER 6

FOCUS YOUR EYES ON TODAY

Many times, when we are in a fight, we say to ourselves, "When will this be over?" "Will this ever end?" I cannot wait until this number of days down the line. The Word says, *"Do not worry about tomorrow, for tomorrow will worry about its own things"* (Matthew 6:34). We try to foolishly manage the future by imagining all types of things that could happen. One of the tactics of the enemy is to make you think you are going to miss out on something if you do not do this or that. You must realize that God holds your future and everything about you is going to get better. You must speak this by faith! Everything in your life must get better! For example, when you first go to college, you must take it one day at a time and one test at a time.

The Word says that *"God will not put more on you than you can bear"*, (1 Corinthians 10:13). God will grace you with the strength and the endurance to finish your race strong. You look up and you are graduating from college after four or five years of hard work and dedication. One thing we must realize is that we live in a microwave society; but it takes time and a process to reach a goal, even though you are fighting with everything you have. For example, you could never tell that a butterfly was once an ugly caterpillar and that it had to fight in the cocoon stage to become a butterfly. Each stage of the butterfly's process was filled with difficulty until it came out to be a beautiful butterfly. I want you to focus on today and watch God come and fight for you in your situation until it comes to pass.

Prayer: *Lord, help me to focus on the now, even though it is hard sometimes. Lord, I know that you are with me always. You said in your Word that you would "never leave me nor forsake me (Deuteronomy 31:8). In Jesus' name. Amen.*

Reflection: What things have I been focusing on?

_____

_____

_____

_____

_____

CHAPTER 7

GIVE YOURSELF AWAY

Y ou are probably asking yourself how you can give yourself away when you are in the fight of your life right now just to survive. We can make it a full-time job feeling sorry for ourselves during our difficult times or we can selflessly give ourselves away to other people. It could be anything small from serving at your church, local food pantry, homeless shelter, or even being a volunteer for an organization in your community that is making a difference in the lives of others. Whatever it may be, make it less about you and more about others. ''Don't look out for only yourself but for the interest of others'' (Philippians 2:4). That sounds crazy when you are in the fight of your life, and it seems like all hope is gone.

We are naturally selfish people and most times, it's all about us. Me! My! Mine! On the contrary, we must realize that someone else's situation is way worse than ours. You can look in the media and see the hundreds of stories of people who have absolutely nothing and still have joy. How can we have this joy during the trial that we are facing? We can find this in Jesus as we look to Him the author and finisher of our faith, who knew no sin but counted it as joy to suffer on the cross, (Hebrew 12:2). Give your life away by praying for others, inviting someone from your church or community over for dinner, or listening to someone who is going through a difficult time. God sees and He knows all. Let God be true and every man a liar concerning your life!

Prayer: *Lord, help me not to always think about me during my struggles and trials, but help me to think of those less fortunate and remember that I have a reason to be thankful for. Help me to give of myself during this battle I am fighting, so you can get the victory in Jesus' name, Amen.*

Reflection: What are some ways I can give myself away? What is stopping me from giving myself away?

CHAPTER 8

OPEN YOUR MOUTH AND SPEAK!

Have you ever heard the heart wrenching noise of a baby crying when they are hungry, needing their diaper changed, or does not feel well? The baby will cry at the top of their little lungs until they get what they want to satisfy their need. That is interesting because as believers some of us are afraid to open our mouths and speak when we are in a battle of our lives. One of the tactics of the enemy is to keep you silent in your head and to make you feel like you are the only one going through that situation. But that is a lie! You must speak to win the victory.

When I played basketball in high school, I would trash talk the best player on the other team to get in his head. I would say things like, "You are not that good," or "I bet you can't dribble with your left hand." Even though physically he could do it, I would get in his mind and that would mess up his game. As believers, we have an enemy who likes to talk lies or half-truth when we are going through situations that seem impossible to get out of. But the weapon we have which can quench every fiery dart of the enemy is the Word of God. The Word says, *"For as he thinks in his heart, so is he"* (Proverbs 23:7). *"Death and life are in the power of the tongue and those who love will eat the fruit of it,"* (Proverbs 18:21). Are you going around saying, "This is terrible! I wonder will this ever end?" Or are you speaking life into the situation. Declare "I will get out of this in the name of Jesus; I am a child of

God, and I will get through this soon." What you meditate on you will eventually come into being. Hebrews 4:12 says that the Word is sharper than any two-edged sword. That is powerful because the truth of the matter is, we cannot speak in our own words because they profit nothing, but the Word is living and powerful.

Some of you may have grown up in a family in which you could not speak up for yourself. The enemy now uses that against you when you are in a situation where you need to open your mouth and speak. We have the choice as believers to speak life to dead situations so they can come back to life. When you are in a fight for your health you say, "By the stripes of Jesus, I am healed." (Isaiah 53:5) When you are in financial need you declare (Philippians 4:13), "And my God shall supply all your need according to His riches in glory by Christ Jesus." The earth is the Lord's and the fullness thereof. (Psalms 24:1) When you are dealing with a broken relationship you declare, "That God will restore everything that the enemy has stolen from you," for God is the healer of the broken heart. (Deuteronomy 30:3) Your words have power! You are not weak, and you can shift the atmosphere that you are in. You can release joy during a trial by declaring that "The joy of the Lord is your strength," according to Nehemiah 8:10. His yoke is easy, and His burden is light. Do not let the enemy keep you silent and have you in mental torment during the storm. You must realize that you will come out of this victorious in Jesus' name. Open your mouth and speak!

Prayer: *Father, I thank you that you have given me the power to speak your Word to be victorious in every situation. Father, help me to realize that I am not a victim and that I have the power to open my mouth and speak to the storms of life. Lord, I trust you that as I read your Word, you will put the Words in my mouth to speak your truth and not the lies of the enemy. In Luke 21:15, you have declared, "For I will give you a mouth and wisdom, which all your adversaries will not be able to contradict or resist." It is so! In Jesus' name, Amen.*

Reflection: What areas in my life do I need to speak the Word of God to?

_____

_____

_____

_____

_____

CONCLUSION

I Pray that this book has encouraged you to keep fighting because God has amazing things in store for your life. It may not feel like it now, but rest assured knowing that "he who has begun a good work in you will complete it until the day of Jesus Christ;" (Philippians 1:9). Put those boxing gloves on and get back in the ring because as a child of God you always come out as the champion. Meditate and let these words of hope encourage you to keep going. The fighter inside of you wants to come out of you during this season but the choice is yours. Lock in and stay focused, and do not let the naysayers make you doubt the promises of God that He has spoken over your life. He has magnificent plans for you, a hope, and a future. No eye has seen the things that God has for those who trust and love Him. (1 Corinthians 2:9).

Remember that our destiny is secure in Jesus if we remain connected to Him. He foreknew us and predestined us for good works. (Ephesians 2:10). You were not born here on accident nor were you a mistake. Consider this! The mere fact that your father was able to fertilize your mother's egg and bring about a conception and miracle called YOU is evidence of itself! Everything about you was the intentionality of God! You are God's chosen possession and God has a wonderful plan for your life. I leave you with this! Remember, this race is not given to the swift nor to the strong but to the one that endures to the very end! The enemy may have caught you off guard, or attempted to take you out, but all is well! Get back in the fight and walk in the victory that is yours! It's time to toe the line, apply pressure, and GET YOUR FIGHT BACK!

ABOUT THE AUTHOR

Roscoe Robinson is a licensed Minister, Author, Social Services Leader, and Public Speaker. He holds a BA in Sociology from the University of Texas at San Antonio and a master's degree in Education from Relay Graduate School of Education. His desire and passion are to see people walk out their God given potential and destiny. Roscoe currently resides in Memphis, TN. He is a member of Divine Life Church Memphis under the leadership of Apostle Tony Wade and Pastor Felicia Wade.

Connect with Roscoe on Social Media.

Facebook: RoscoeRobinsonGlobal

Instagram: RoscoejRobinson

Made in the USA
Columbia, SC
26 November 2022

71830354R00030